Stocks Are Simple!

A Beginner's Learning Guide

Volume 2:

Stock Picking 101

Written by: Jenice Dennis

Stocks Are Simple! A Beginner's Learning Guide Volume 2 © Copyright <<2020>> Jenice Dennis

All rights reserved. No part of this publication may be reproduced, distributed, or transmitted in any form or by any means, including photocopying, recording, or other electronic or mechanical methods, without the prior written permission of the publisher, except in the case of brief quotations embodied in critical reviews and certain other noncommercial uses permitted by copyright law.

Although the author and publisher have made every effort to ensure that the information in this book was correct at press time, the author and publisher do not assume and hereby disclaim any liability to any party for any loss, damage, or disruption caused by errors or omissions, whether such errors or omissions result from negligence, accident, or any other cause.

Adherence to all applicable laws and regulations, including international, federal, state, and local governing professional licensing, business practices, advertising, and all other aspects of doing business in the US, Canada, or any other jurisdiction is the sole responsibility of the reader and consumer.

Neither the author nor the publisher assumes any responsibility or liability whatsoever on behalf of the consumer or reader of this material. Any perceived slight of any individual or organization is purely unintentional.

The resources in this book are provided for informational purposes only and should not be used to replace the specialized training and professional judgment of a legal or tax professional. Neither the author nor the publisher can be held responsible for the use of the information provided within this book. Please always consult a trained professional before making any decision regarding your financial situation.

The advice and strategies found within may not be suitable for every situation. This work is sold with the understanding that neither the author nor the publisher is held responsible for the results accrued from the advice in this book.

For more information, email Jenice@investsimplenow.com

GET YOUR FREE GIFT!

The purchase of this book comes with a gift!

To get the best experience with this book, I've found that readers who download and use my FREE Stock Journal are able to learn quicker, implement faster, and take the next steps needed to get started in the stock market.

You can get a copy by visiting:

www.investsimplenow.com

Join the mailing list to be notified once the next books of this series are published.

Table of Contents

Introduction 5

Chapter 1: *How to determine the goal of your portfolio* 7

Chapter 1 Review 11

Chapter 2: *How to pick stocks in different market conditions* ..15

Chapter 2 Review 21

Chapter 3: *How to analyze a stock using the NASDAQ dozen grading system* 26

Chapter 3 Review 32

Chapter 4: *What are the best strategies that investors and traders use to pick stock?* 36

Chapter 4 Review 40

Author Bio 45

Introduction

Even the most knowledgeable investors may make the mistake of picking stocks that do not make sense for their portfolio, causing unnecessary loss. This is why many investors go for balance in their portfolio by diversifying their investments. Developing clear-cut stock-picking strategies will allow investors to spot great opportunities in the market, minimize possible loss, and strengthen their portfolio. Many people do not know that investment portfolios are used to measure net worth and help offset liabilities. This makes the stocks you invest in all the more important. How cool would it be to possibly have a net worth of hundreds of thousands of dollars just for investing or trading intelligently? This is certainly more achievable than many people believe, as it has been achieved by many and may soon be achieved by you.

Picking a stock is all about researching and striking when the iron is hot. It may seem tiring to go over multiple finance documents for several companies and read article after article while keeping an ear on the news, all to gather the most information possible to make the best trades and investments that you can, but learning about the stock market and the industries within is learning about our very economy at its core which is not a bad thing. As a matter of fact, it may even open your eyes to being financially literate and help you to manage your finances better as a whole. Knowledge is power!

No matter how you spin it, you cannot go wrong with investing and trading as long as you pick the stocks that match your goals and stick to the plans you create. Personally, my biggest struggle starting in the market was picking stocks based on research and not emotion. Simply because I thought if I invested in staple companies that I loved, I would clearly always see positive returns, and boy was I wrong. The first few times that I noticed I picked a bad stock taught me not to jump into investing without proper research on a company, especially if the company doesn't have much reported information available to begin with. We will explore and work around obstacles to find the best way to pick the best possible stocks for the best possible outcome. This book will be the stock-picking guide to kick start your journey of being a master stock picker!

Chapter 1:

How to determine the goal of your portfolio

Before you begin to stock up on stocks, be sure that you are clear on what you'd like to accomplish with your portfolio in the long-term. You need to take the time to do this to ensure that you position yourself to assume the amount of risk that you can handle, especially working with what you can handle during the time frame set for the goals that you need to reach. Doing this will take trial and error by way of adjusting the amount of each asset you own to reflect the goals that you have set for your portfolio. The determination of your **investment portfolio** type and said investment portfolio's performance depends on your **asset allocation**. Seeing as though your portfolio is an overall outlook of the assets that you own, such as stocks, bonds, mutual funds, and other securities. The mix of securities you own will determine whether your investment portfolio is super **conservative** or highly **aggressive**. Neither is bad; it all depends on the type of investor you would like to be. You may also revamp your portfolio whenever you feel a change in direction is needed. Always remember to use caution and go in with a plan for anything you do in the market to avoid costly mistakes. In this series, we are concentrating on individual stocks; therefore, if you choose to begin solely investing in individual stocks, such as I did, then your portfolio will be considered high risk and very aggressive.

With a very aggressive and high-risk portfolio, an investor is investing in individual stocks more than any other security or solely in individual stocks.

These investors have high hopes for the longevity of the companies they invest in and believe in the swings of the market. To these investors, the swings of the market will cause what goes up to come back down, but also, these investors believe that what goes down may very well come back up. If you are invested in the right companies, then the stock will experience downtrends a few times over the years but will regain strength, surpass previous highs, and stabilize as time goes on. That is what drives these investors to maintain aggressive portfolios for many years. The main purpose of this type of portfolio is **capital growth** by selecting companies that have a history or a very good chance of growing each year at an impressive rate. Basically, investors with this type of portfolio are looking to attain a very high profit of returns with compounding dividends and the possible growth of their investment in the long-term. This makes their portfolio very volatile throughout the years, but these investors will not fear this volatility. Always remember the higher the risk, the higher the reward.

A step beneath having a very aggressive portfolio is having an aggressive portfolio with medium risk. In this portfolio, you will achieve more balance in your portfolio than a very aggressive portfolio while still carrying a bigger percentage of individual stocks over other investments. The beauty of this portfolio is investing in other securities such as bonds, money markets, and so on, more than a very aggressive investor would, which will help you to level out possible loss and still see a high return of profits. This would be a great portfolio for younger investors as they will reap the benefits of having very aggressive investments that will possibly see great growth year after year while also being safe with conservative investments to ensure some form of a return is made.

Whereas someone who invests primarily in fixed-income securities such as certain bonds while also investing in a few aggressive assets such as individual stocks will have a portfolio that is considered medium risk and conservative. These types of portfolios are great if you would like to spend a shorter time in the market and make a decent return of profits. These conservative investors add individual stocks to their portfolios to offset **inflation** in their portfolios. This is great because using the equity from certain investments to invest in other investments keeps your wealth-building itself overtime and protects you from inflation on your investments, which sabotages your return of profits. An example is making a return profit of 10% on a bond, but let's say inflation went up 5% over the years as well. This drops your return of profits from 10% profit to just 5% profit. Would you rather take that 5% out of the market and assume a 5% loss or invest that 5% in another investment type that is a bit more aggressive and watch your money grow that way? The second option sounds better to me!

Very conservative and low-risk investors use the same method as conservative investors to invest in mostly or solely fixed-income securities and offset inflation in their portfolio with blue-chip individual stocks as well. The difference is that very conservative investors hold their aggressive assets at a lower percentage in their portfolio than a conservative investor. Figuring out which will work best for you is reliant on your risk tolerance. Case in point, if you are a bit older and closer to retirement and are looking to grow your money in a shorter amount of time with no or not much risk involved, then a very conservative low-risk portfolio would be best for you. These types of portfolios allow for **capital preservation** seeing as most of your investments will pay out interest payments as the security is maturing. Once matured, you stand to recoup your initial investment. That is what makes this strategy appealing to some investors because it's the closest you can get to really making sure you leave the market with a profit even if it is not as high of a return as an aggressive investor stands to make.

Needless to say, you could potentially make investing an almost exact science, which will only make the process that much more straight-forward and goal-oriented, therefore being simpler for you to execute. This is a great way to drive results and see the return of profits you are aiming for with your chosen portfolio type. Once you are welled versed and confident in the portfolio you would like to create, you may begin researching the companies that you would like to fill the said portfolio with. Be sure to calculate how much to invest in each investment type to reach the percentages you've set forth. This allows for strategic investing and lends a hand to your investment portfolio's success and the returns that you make.

Chapter 1 Review

Key Terms:

Aggressive portfolio: a portfolio that consists mainly of individual stocks. Usually has a medium to high-risk level.

Asset allocation: the different percentages of assets you own in each investment type used to determine the risk level of your investment portfolio.

Capital growth: the increase of your investment over the time that you are invested. A strategy often used in aggressive portfolios.

Capital preservation: the preservation of your investment by guaranteeing returns and minimizing loss. A strategy often used in conservative portfolios.

Conservative portfolio: a portfolio that consists mainly of fixed-income securities such as bonds. Usually has a medium to low-risk level.

Inflation: the decrease in the value of money.

Investment portfolio: houses the mix of securities an investor owns.

Chapter 1 Review Test

1) What is the purpose of having an asset allocation plan?

   _____

   _____

2) Investing solely in individual stocks will lead to what type of portfolio?
   A) Conservative
   B) Very aggressive
   C) Aggressive
   D) Very Conservative

3) Capital growth is accomplished by exclusively investing in fixed income securities. **(True or False)**

4) A portfolio with medium risk that mostly focuses on fixed income investments is known as a _____ portfolio.

5) What portfolio has the lowest amount of risk? _____.

6) What is capital preservation? _____

   _____.

Chapter 1 Worksheet

Date: _____

Research and fill in this worksheet to create a goal for your portfolio.

Portfolio goals:

My portfolio will be (Very conservative, conservative, Aggressive, Very aggressive)

Risk tolerance: (Low, Medium, High)

I will accomplish this goal by:

1) _____

   (Ex: Diversifying my investment types)

2) _____

3) _____

4) _____

5) _____

Asset Allocation practice: Research the common asset allocation for the portfolio you chose and use this as a guide when you are ready to invest.

_____% Stocks

_____% Bonds

_____% ETFs

_____% Mutual Funds

_____% _____ (Fill in with another investment type)

Notes:

Chapter 2:

How to pick stocks in different market conditions

The stock market experiences different market conditions based on economic factors that affect many companies at the same time, such as inflation. To understand the stock market and the different ways it may present itself at any given moment, let's get a bit deeper into how the stock market works at its core. Essentially, the stock market is comprised of a **primary market** and a **secondary market**. In the primary market, companies offer shares of their company for the first time to the public in what's called an **initial public offering**, mostly referenced to as an **IPO**. The company does this to raise capital for the business to accomplish projects that will generate more profits. After the initial public offering, the company now has its capital and will go off to work on the projects that needed funding. Meanwhile, the investors that initially invested now own all of the stock that the company put on the market; therefore, those investors may decide to sell their shares to new buyers interested in owning shares of that company on the secondary market. The secondary market is mainly everything I've described in Volume 1 of this series.

There are many investors who mainly invest in IPO's, seeing as they have a greater chance of getting a good value on the company. These investors will be among the first to own the company; therefore, if the demand for the stock rises, the price may sky-rocket and allow the initial investors to make amazing profit returns whenever they decide to sell. You have a better chance of seeing higher returns if you purchase IPO's, but keep in mind that the opposite may happen, and the company could possibly not make any head way as you expected it to, leaving you stuck with the company until it starts to make gains. Horribly, they could never see any real gains or even go bankrupt shortly after the company enters the market if the company doesn't get many investors or make much revenue. A great way to find and research upcoming IPO's is to check websites like Yahoo Finance or search for websites that track IPO's online. Once you locate an IPO that you are interested in, whether it be because you know much about the company already, have heard that good things are to come of that company, or whatever the reason for your interest, you will need to do thorough research before deciding which IPO's to pick by looking at the company's strengths, weaknesses, opportunities for growth, and potential threats such as competitors. New companies, as well as established companies, may be IPO's because many established companies prefer to remain private until it's necessary to become public. Personally, I only invest in an IPO if it is a well-established company that I am familiar with simply because that makes me most comfortable, and these companies typically have more data to go off of.

Next, let's go over the different **market trends** you will see in the stock market. The first is an **uptrend,** which as the name states, is when stock prices are trending upwards. This is usually due to the demand for investing in the market growing. The best way to recognize when the stock market is in an uptrend is noticing that prices are getting higher and stabilizing at higher prices than normal. Although the prices may drop a bit, which is normal and expected, the prices do not fall below the previous low prices.

For example, if my company's stock is trading at a price anywhere between $40 - $50 consistently for some time, then I release finance documents that show an increase of earnings for my company with projections to earn more. This will cause investors to become interested in my stock, subsequently driving the stock price further up. Now my company is trading at a price range of $80 - $90 and never falls below the previous low price during the time that it is trending upwards; this is considered the stock being in an uptrend. Apply this to the majority of the stock market rising in the same manner, then that will showcase that the stock market is in an uptrend.

When the market is in an uptrend, investors believe that the stock prices will continue to move up until eventually leveling out to a certain price range. Using this logic, **bullish investors**, investors who believe in the market or a certain stock, invest as much as possible and will pick stocks that are in an uptrend as a way to profit off the increasing stock prices. Short-term investors such as day traders and swing traders will sell when the prices have reached their peak, causing the prices to drop as they sell their shares along with long-term investors who have been with the company for many years and are ready to reap the rewards. These traders are often the reason why the market enters into a **downtrend**.

A downtrend is when stock prices are trending downward and hitting lows lower than previous lows, even if not the lowest price that the stock has ever been. Taking from the previous example, if instead, my company's finance reports show a decrease in earnings and investors no longer believe in my company sustaining high prices or growing, they will then sell their shares and cause the stock to fall. Once applied to the market as a whole, the market will see many stock prices fall and could become a bear market. A bear market occurs when **bearish investors**, investors who **short sell** shares of a stock believing the stock price will eventually fall, begin to sell shares due to believing the company or the stock market is no longer going to sustain highs. The stock prices begin to fall to the point where once again, bullish investors will see the low prices as a discount and start to invest again, causing a bull market. This will cause the prices to rise back up and possibly enter into another uptrend. The stock market is essentially the repeating of these trends over and over.

Investors may also be a plethora of titles as the market changes, just like the stock market is a plethora of different conditions. Never think that you are only a bullish investor or a bearish investor; you may be either at any moment, even if you are predominantly one over the other. The overall direction of the stock market dictates what investors have to be, do, and believe to make the best decisions possible to increase their investments in the time frame the investor is seeking.

Once in a downtrend, the stock market may crash if investors continue to sell more than they buy. This is usually due to economic changes or some sort of major crisis that will cause the market to go down rapidly and unexpectedly, making investors panic. Once many investors have panicked and sold their shares, this leaves the market in a depressed state. This means that investors who chose not to sell shares will see a decline in their profit margins during this time. The great thing about savvy investors is that they are aware that the market can correct itself; therefore, they leave their investments alone as well as buy more shares to add to the value of their investments as these investors believe the prices will rise again one day. These investors pick stocks based on the low price position in conjunction with what they believe the high price could potentially be when the crash is over.

There have been many well-known **stock market crashes** that were publicized and caused many people to fear investing and solidified that they would never do it because of the horror stories that they've heard of people losing incredible amounts of money. Personally, I was not invested during those times, but if I were, I believe I would have handled it just as I am with the current stock market crash that we are experiencing in 2020 due to the global pandemic, which is by holding on to my investments, seeing as I am only invested in companies that I believe would survive a crash, and purchasing more shares of said companies. I believe that I do this because my logic seems to be that many billionaires, politicians, and companies depend on the income made in the stock market; therefore, potentially, they would never allow the market to crash too badly if they have any control, which has been proven by the market being stimulated by the government and other entities during the current pandemic. Keep in mind during stock market crashes that not all stocks are falling. Some sectors may be affected terribly by a crash while other sectors flourish beautifully. It depends on what is causing the crash.

Realistically, not every company will regrow after a stock market crash, but the stock market as a whole is known to bounce back. A **stock market correction** takes place over many months or just a few weeks, depending on how bad the dip was as investors begin to invest again. It could take several years as it has for the stock crashes that have happened previously. If you are a long-term investor, then this will not scare you because you've planned for this and have the patience for the market to be better. On the other hand, if you are a trader, this could hinder you from profiting from your planned trades, causing you to potentially lose money or forcing you into a long-term position.

All in all, being able to identify the many different stock market conditions gives you even more clarity on what stocks to pick during these constantly changing times. The fact that the market does change so frequently also adds an element to your duties of researching and making educated decisions because even big companies may not survive a crash or may lose a ton of value and never regain it. There are many strategies used to pick stocks in any market condition; let's go over those next.

Chapter 2 Review

Key Terms:

Bearish investors: expects the price of shares to fall; therefore, they short sell stocks.

Bullish investors: expects the price of shares to rise; therefore, they buy stocks.

Downtrend: occurs when stock prices drop lower than previous lows.

Initial public offering: when a company decides to offer shares of their company to the public for the first time.

Market trends: the directions in which the market tends to move.

Primary market: where companies enter the stock market with an IPO.

Secondary market: where shares are bought and sold after an IPO.

Short sell: borrowing stocks to sell and then buying them back when the prices have dropped.

Stock market correction: occurs when stock prices shift 10% but less than 20% for a period of time, usually a few months.

Stock market crash: occurs when stock prices drop over 10% in a single day.

Uptrend: occurs when stock prices rise higher than previous highs.

Chapter 2 Review Test

1) An IPO takes place in a secondary market. **(True or False)**

2) An investor that short sells stock is known as a bullish investor. **(True or False)**

3) What is the difference between an uptrend and downtrend?
_____
_____

4) What is a bear market? _____
_____.

5) What happens in a stock market crash?
_____.

6) What happens in a stock market correction?
_____.

Chapter 2 Worksheet

Date: _____

Research and fill in this worksheet to practice identifying market trends.

Current market trend: _____

Current crash or correction: _____

Sectors that are currently up: _____

Sectors that are currently down: _____

Companies in the sectors that are currently up that I am interested in investing in or trading are: (Stock tickers)

1) _____ 2) _____ 3) _____

Companies in the sectors that are currently down that I am interested in investing in or trading are: (Stock tickers)

1) _____ 2) _____ 3) _____

Practice: Pretend you have ten thousand dollars to invest in one company that is currently up and another ten thousand to invest in a company that is down. Write the stock ticker, current price, and the number of shares. In two months, check those companies again and evaluate what has happened with the market and your pretend investments.

Company A (up): _____ Price: _____ # of shares: _____ two-month price: _____

Company B (down): _____ Price: _____ # of shares: _____ two-month price: _____

Notes:

Chapter 3:

How to analyze a stock using the NASDAQ dozen grading system

There are many different ways that investors analyze a stock before they make a solid decision to invest. My personal favorite way to research and analyze a stock is using the NASDAQ dozen grading system. Although the NASDAQ grading system has been bumped up to seventeen steps, I recommend the original twelve steps because they are easy and efficient enough, in my opinion. Seeing as I am mainly a long-term investor, following this grading system allows me to get information on all of the important factors of a company and a clearer picture of where the company may be headed in the future. This is important because you will be much more confident in your investment decisions by picking stocks that align with your goals for the time frame you've set forth. Let's talk about each step and how investors grade the stock overall.

The first step to analyzing a stock using this grading system is to research the company's revenue. A company's revenue is important because you want to invest in profitable companies that will continue to grow and be profitable as time goes on. The way you will grade a company's revenue is by comparing the company's annual revenue from the prior year or two to the current year, if possible. If the company shows increasing revenue annually, give them a passing score for this factor. You may even compare the most recent completed quarter of the current year to the same quarter of the previous year, and once again, if revenue shows an increase, then give the company a pass. If the revenue for the company is instead decreasing, give the company a fail.

The next step is to analyze the **earnings per share** or **EPS** of the company. In analyzing this, investors are able to determine how much of the profit shareholders will receive as a result of the company's growing revenue. The more profits investors stand to make per share, the more valuable they become to other investors, allowing the stock price to rise. If the company's earnings per share is increasing annually or by quarter, as stated in step one, you may give them a pass for this factor. If the EPS is decreasing instead, you will give the company a fail.

Return on equity or **ROE** is the next factor we take a look into. ROE will indicate to investors how a company is generating profits for shareholders based on the amount of equity in the company. To calculate return on equity, you simply take the average of shareholder equity from the last year and divide it by the net profit that the company has made during the same year. If ROE is increasing for the last two years, give this factor a pass. If ROE is decreasing for the last two years, give this factor a fail.

Professional opinion is very important in financial matters because you may know a lot on your own, but as humans, we naturally tend to act on emotion or think that whatever we believe is the end all be all, which is why analyst recommendations are the next factor that investors will research. The professional analyst will do thorough research on the company and announce whether to buy into the stock, hold the stock, or sell the stock based on their findings and the company's possible future direction. If overall analysts agree that a stock is a strong buy or buy, then give this factor a pass. If analysts are recommending anything less than to buy the stock, then give this factor a fail.

This next factor also involves professional analyst predictions, and it's referenced as positive earnings surprises. Positive earnings surprises occur when a company reveals its earnings, and analyst make guesses about what the investors will earn once those company earnings begin to trickle down to the shareholders. Analysts are essentially guessing what the EPS will be; therefore, it is a positive surprise if the EPS is higher than what the analyst predicted. Seeing as companies announce their earnings quarterly, if the earnings per share surprises show to be positive for the last four completed quarters, give this factor a pass. Give this factor a fail if any of the four quarters were negative.

Analysts will also give out earnings forecasts for companies because knowing a company's past EPS is great, but you also want to have an idea of future earnings to be made. This way, investors can gauge if a company has reached its peak or has the ability to be increasingly profitable. If analysts give an EPS forecast that increases yearly, give this factor a pass. If the EPS forecast decreases, give this factor a fail.

The next factor to analyze is earnings growth, which is also predicted by professional analysts. In this factor, analysts will make predictions as to what the company's earnings will be per year for the next five years based on past research as well as future products, services, or announcements from said company. Investors can use this information to get an idea of what a long-term position would look like in the company. If the analysts give the company's stock a five-year growth percentage of 8% or more, give this factor a pass. If the growth shows to be less than 8%, give this factor a fail.

PEG ratio is used to determine a company's overall growth by using the company's price to earnings ratio, or P/E ratio. Analysts will calculate this ratio by dividing the P/E ratio by the rate of growth that is expected within a year for the company. If the PEG ratio value is less than 1.0, give this factor a pass. If the value is more than 1.0, give this factor a fail.

To make sure the company we are looking to invest in is actually performing well, investors will look at industry price-earnings, which reveal the earnings that the average company in that industry makes. In doing this, investors are able to gauge whether this company is a front runner in the industry or falling behind. If the company's earnings are higher than the industry earnings are, then give this factor a pass. If lower, give this factor a fail.

Days to cover is the next factor to analyze. Days to cover involves short-term investors and the possibility of them covering their positions in the short-term. It is the number of days it will take to cover short positions in a stock based on the average trading volume of said stock. If days to cover shows to be less than 2 days, give this factor a pass. If more than two days, give this factor a fail.

We have all heard about insider trading by now and the eggshells around it. **Insider trading** is when you notice people inside of the company are buying into the stock, usually based on insider information. If the company management themselves are confident in the ability of the stock to make money, this, in turn, increases investors' excitement and causes investors to invest into the company as well. If net activity with inside traders has been positive for the last three months, give this factor a pass. If the net activity has been negative for the last three months, give this factor a fail.

The goal of purchasing a stock is to watch your investment increase and make amazing profits. That is why investors' last step in this NASDAQ grading system is to check the weighted alpha of a stock. In checking this, investors may determine if a stock price is moving higher or lower. Weighted alpha measures a year of stock price movement, which is how analysts are able to determine whether the price will go up or down. If the weighted alpha is a positive number, that means the stock price is moving higher, and you may give this factor a pass. If the weighted alpha is a negative number, give this factor a fail.

Those were the original twelve NASDAQ grading factors. To research these items for the companies that you are interested in, you may use the NASDAQ official website or any similar website to it. Once you have all the grades for each factor, you want to give the stock an overall score as a way to determine if you should invest or not. The rule of thumb is that if the company scores 12 passes and 0 fails to 9 passes and 3 fails, or anywhere between 12:0 – 9:3, then the company is a strong buy and could potentially be a strong candidate for continued growth in the market. If the score is between 8:4 to 6:6, then the company is a moderate buy and a moderate candidate for growth. Any score below 6:6 shows that the company is not a great buy and will most likely be a poor candidate for growth. All in all, using this grading system will help you to make the best choices for your investments and give you a better chance of turning amazing profits!

Chapter 3 Review

Key Terms:

Earnings per share or **EPS:** measures the amount of profits that the company makes for each share of stock.

Insider trading: the act of buying shares based on insiders also buying shares of their company's stock.

Return on equity or **ROE:** measures the amount of return profits a company is able to generate for shareholders based on equity.

Chapter 3 Review Test

1) Revenue must be increasing yearly or quarterly to receive a passing score. **(True or False)**

2) The factor that helps determine the profit shareholders may receive per share from company earnings is:
A) PEG ratio
B) EPS
C) ROE

3) You should automatically invest in stocks that analysts give a buy rating or higher. **(True or False)**

4) How do you calculate the PEG ratio of a company?
_____.

5) What is insider trading?
_____.

6) What scores are considered to be poor after you finish grading the stock? _____.

Chapter 3 Worksheet

Date: _____

Research and fill in this worksheet to practice using the NASDAQ dozen to grade stocks.

Practice: Pick one stock and fill in the information below to determine if the stock is worth being added to your portfolio.

Stock ticker: _____   Stock price: _____

Revenue: PASS OR FAIL

Earnings per share: PASS OR FAIL

Return on Equity: PASS OR FAIL

Analyst Recommendations: PASS OR FAIL

Positive Earnings Surprise: PASS OR FAIL

Earnings Forecast: PASS OR FAIL

Earnings Growth: PASS OR FAIL

PEG Ratio: PASS OR FAIL

Industry price-earnings: PASS OR FAIL

Days to cover: PASS OR FAIL

Insider trading: PASS OR FAIL

Weighted Alpha: PASS OR FAIL

Final Score: _____

Notes:

Chapter 4:

What are the best strategies that investors and traders use to pick stock?

A long-term investor is looking for different qualities than a short-term investor. Don't get me wrong, it starts the same, but long-term investors are looking for slow and steady growth, where-as short-term investors are more interested in fast-moving stock prices in order to make money in the nearer future. The technique described above, the NASDAQ dozen, may be used by both types of investors though mainly used by long-term investors.

Long-term investors should definitely start with the NASDAQ dozen strategy and use that method on **blue-chip stocks** to pick the best stocks for their long-term goals. If the stock gets a final passing grade, I personally look into what the stock price currently is compared to what I believe would be a great lower price for the stock. Consequently, I set an alert for somewhere in the middle of those two prices unless I feel the company will be rising and may not drop to that lower price. In that case, I would just invest immediately at the given price not to miss out on the rising stock price. By the way, my online broker allows me to set alerts for when prices are falling or rising to alert me to decide whether to buy or sell.

Let's say a new long-term investor is interested in investing in Amazon, and after grading Amazon using the NASDAQ dozen grading system, the investor finds out that Amazon is a strong candidate for growth. Suppose the investor feels that Amazon is a great candidate for growth, but after reviewing Amazon's chart, the investor realized that Amazon takes a **dip** every two weeks. In that case, that investor may decide to wait for the next dip if they believe there will be one. Investors can do this by placing an alert at the price they wish to own the stock or placing an order for the price they wish to own the stock. We will discuss how to place orders thoroughly and utilize other helpful tools in the next book of this series. Once alerted, the investor can purchase the stock at the lower price. The flip side is if the investor feels the stock price is already acceptable or may not go back down for a while or at all, then the investor will invest immediately. To keep it simple for beginners, utilize these methods for your long-term investments mixed with the short-term strategy we will discuss now.

Although I recommend the NASDAQ dozen grading system mainly for long-term investors, short-term investors should utilize that strategy as well, especially for trades they plan to enact over a period of time. A popular strategy that traders employ is finding the pivot points of a stock to determine support and resistance levels, to plan an entry and exit, and create risk management orders such as a stop-loss order, a take-profit order, or a limit-order.

Going back to book one, where we discussed daily and weekly pivot points being used by day and swing traders, you may even find monthly pivot points for the stock as a long-term investor to keep track of where the stock direction is headed. These pivot points are used to determine when a trader should open a position (buy) and when they should close a position (sell). Pivot points are found by using the average of the previous high, low, and close stock price to estimate the price's direction to examine when to buy and sell shares. As an example, an investor is interested in trading Amazon as a day trade. The investor will check Amazon's high, low, and close price for the previous day to see where the stock could potentially be at the best price of the next day in order to buy low and then sell high within the same trading day. This would require a lot of capital for this particular company, but you may use this strategy on small **market capitalization** stocks to mid-size companies that show prospects of hitting it big or anywhere in between as long as you do the proper research.

Once the pivot point has been determined, the trader will use that to predict where the stock will have support and resistance to plan an entry and exit strategy for said stock. To do this, traders will complete several equations to find the levels they are looking for. To find the first support level, traders will take the determined pivot point and multiply that by two, and then subtract the previous day's high from the answer. Next, find the second support level by subtracting the previous day's low from the previous day's high and then subtracting the answer from the pivot point that was determined. Once you have the pivot point, support level one, and support level two, it is now time to find the resistance levels.

To find the first resistance level of a stock, traders will multiply the pivot point by two and subtract the previous low from the answer. Next, find the second resistance level by subtracting the previous day's low from the previous day's high and then adding the answer to the determined pivot point. Now that you have all of your points, you will have an idea of what you may profit the day you employ what you've researched. Keep in mind that these are just predictive points to help you plan when to buy and sell for the best profit possible.

Traders know exactly how to execute their orders so that they may do so swiftly and as close to perfect as possible, limiting the amount of risk they are assuming as best as they can. This is why I mentioned the creation of risk management by placing limit-orders, etc. that will essentially minimize the damage if a trade goes wrong. The next book of this series is where we will go over exactly how they do it!

These strategies are great and easy for beginners to get started towards making better decisions when choosing a stock to invest in or trade. Once you've mastered these and have seen growth as a result, you may decide to develop your own strategies or research others.

Chapter 4 Review

Key Terms:

Blue-chip stocks: large established companies that have been around many years with a great reputation, solid earnings, and usually pay dividends.

Dip: when the stock falls by no more than 10%.

Market capitalization: the total value of a company's shares of stock, used to measure the size and value of a company.

Chapter 4 Review Test

1) What are blue-chip stocks?

_____.

2) A dip is worse than a stock market crash. **(True or False)**

3) Traders use pivot points to: 1) _____.
   2) _____.
   3) _____.

4) How do traders find support level one?

_____.

5) What prices do you use to determine the average pivot point?

_____.

6) What is market capitalization?

_____.

Chapter 4 Worksheet

Date: _____

Research and fill in this worksheet to practice stock picking.

Find 5 blue-chip stocks and perform NASDAQ dozen.

Stock tickers: Final score: Did you invest:

_____   _____   _____

_____   _____   _____

_____   _____   _____

_____   _____   _____

_____   _____   _____

Find one small market capitalization stock and research the pivot points.

Find the pivot points for _____ on the day of _____.
                              (Ex: Stock Ticker)   (Date researched)

Previous day's High: Low: Close:

Pivot point (Average):

Next, find the support & resistance levels by using the equations described in chapter 4.

Support level one: Support level two:

Resistance level one: Resistance level two:

Finally, watch the stock the next trading day and note whether the stock hit the pivot points you found.

Notes:

Read more!!!

The next book of this series is all about conducting transactions in the stock market. This book will help you to ensure that you are well-equipped to process successful transactions in the stock market confidently!

Author Bio

Jenice Dennis is a millennial investor who has garnered years of experience in the stock market as she began at what is normally considered a young age. Growing up, Jenice did not hear much about investing in her Caribbean household like many other millennials of all backgrounds due to the once exclusive nature of the market and the flat-out fear of investing. Jenice began her journey with a limited budget and no guidance, but with proper research and determination, she has seen exponential growth in her portfolio and wants to share her knowledge with those who need a simple way to get started investing in the market confidently. By removing the intimidating mask of the stock market and breaking it down to a school level type education, Jenice hopes this book and those to come of this series find their way into the hands of Gen Z-ers, millennials, and baby boomers alike and change their lives for the better.

www.ingramcontent.com/pod-product-compliance
Lightning Source LLC
Chambersburg PA
CBHW081704220526
45466CB00009B/2874